Celebrations

Let's Get Ready for Memorial Day

By Lloyd G. Douglas

Children's Press®
A Division of Scholastic Inc.
New York / Toronto / London / Auckland / Sydney
Mexico City / New Delhi / Hong Kong
Danbury, Connecticut

Photo Credits: Cover and all photos by Maura B. McConnell
Contributing Editor: Jennifer Silate
Book Design: Daniel Hosek

Library of Congress Cataloging-in-Publication Data

Douglas, Lloyd G.
    Let's get ready for Memorial Day / by Lloyd G. Douglas.
    p. cm. — (Celebrations)
    Summary: A girl's class prepares for Memorial Day by learning about the
    holiday from their teacher and making flags, and later she goes to a war
    memorial with her father to honor those who died.
    Includes index.
    ISBN 0-516-24263-6 (lib. bdg.) — ISBN 0-516-24355-1 (pbk.)
    1. Memorial Day,—Juvenile literature. [1. Memorial Day. 2. Holidays.]
    I. Title. II. Celebrations (Children's Press)

    E642 .D68 2003
    394.262—dc21
                                                    2002011321

Contents

My name is Amy.

My class is getting ready for **Memorial Day**.

My teacher tells us that on Memorial Day we remember the people who have died in **wars**.

MEMORIAL
DAY
WRITING TO PERSUADE
Incorporate Advertising Techniques
Include Supporting Details
Use a Positive Tone
Answer Potential Objections
Persuasive Writing Includes
OPINION
SUPER CLEANING!
AT THE MOVIES

We are making American flags for Memorial Day.

We use red and blue **markers** to make our flags.

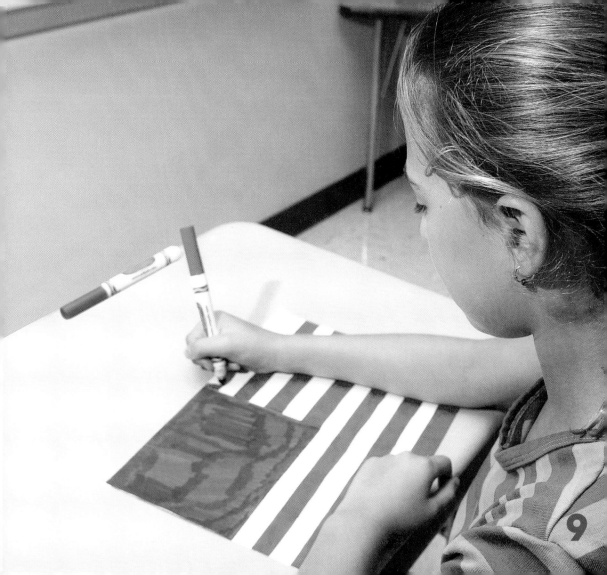

The American flag has fifty stars.

I put stars on my flag.

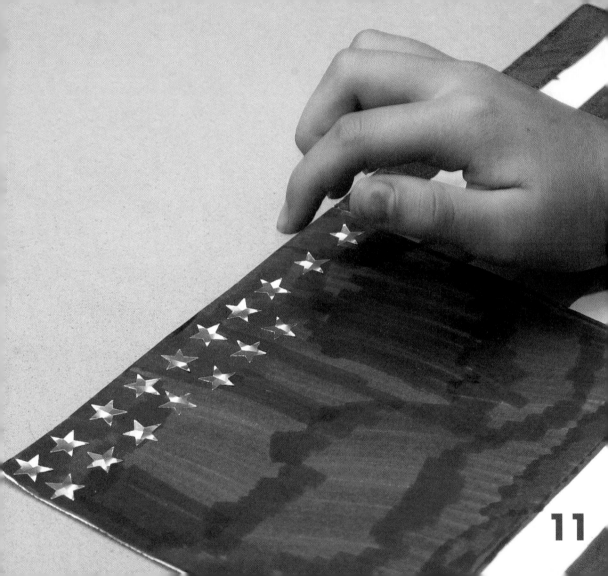

Look at the **calendar**.

Today is Memorial Day.

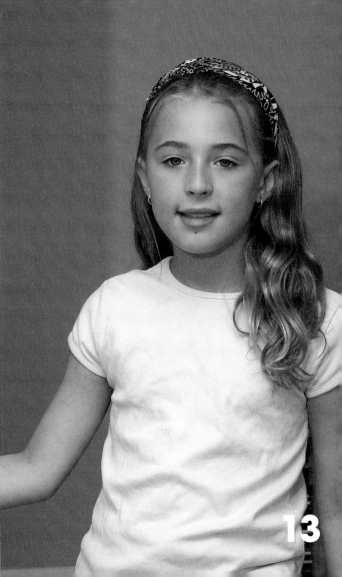

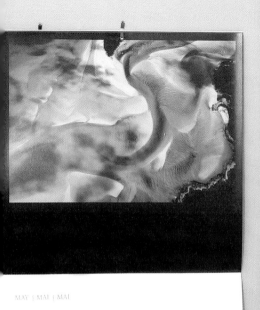

Dad and I are going to a **war memorial** to **celebrate** Memorial Day.

I bring the flag I made.

Dad brings flowers.

The war memorial was made to remember the people who died in wars.

The names of many people are written on the memorial.

THIS MEMORIAL WAS ERECTED EXCLUSIVELY THROUGH THE
VOLUNTEER EFFORTS AND GENEROUS CONTRIBUTIONS OF
THE CITIZENS OF THE DELAWARE VALLEY AREA. TO THOSE
WHO HAVE HELPED, THE PHILADELPHIA VIETNAM VETERANS
MEMORIAL FUND EXTENDS ITS SINCERE APPRECIATION.

IT HAS BEEN AN HONOR AND PRIVILEGE TO SERVE

THE MEMORIAL FUND
JEST RE-TIGH 1962 OCTOBER 26, 1987

17

I leave my flag at
the memorial.

Dad leaves his flowers.

We will always remember the people who died in wars.

New Words

calendar (**kal**-uhn-dur) a chart showing all the days, weeks, and months in a year

celebrate (**sel**-uh-brate) to do something enjoyable on a special occasion

markers (**mahr**-kuhrz) pens with colored ink

Memorial Day (muh-**mor**-ee-uhl **day**) a holiday celebrated in the United States on the last Monday of May to honor Americans who have died in wars

war memorial (**wor** muh-**mor**-ee-uhl) something that is built or done to help people continue to remember the people who died in wars

wars (**worz**) fighting between the armies of different countries or between groups of people in the same country

22

To Find Out More

Books
Memorial Day
by Helen Frost
Pebble Books

Memorial Day
by Mir Tamim Ansary
Heineman Library

Web Site
U.S. Memorial Day History and Information on U.S. War Memorials
http://www.usmemorialday.org
This Web site has Memorial Day e-cards, activities, and information
about the history of the holiday.

Index

About the Author
Lloyd G. Douglas is an editor and writer of children's books.

Reading Consultants
Kris Flynn, Coordinator, Small School District Literacy, The San Diego County Office of Education

Shelly Forys, Certified Reading Recovery Specialist, W.J. Zahnow Elementary School, Waterloo, IL

Sue McAdams, Former President of the North Texas Reading Council of the IRA, and Early Literacy Consultant, Dallas, TX